STATE PROFILES

RHODE ISLAND

BY BETSY RATHBURN

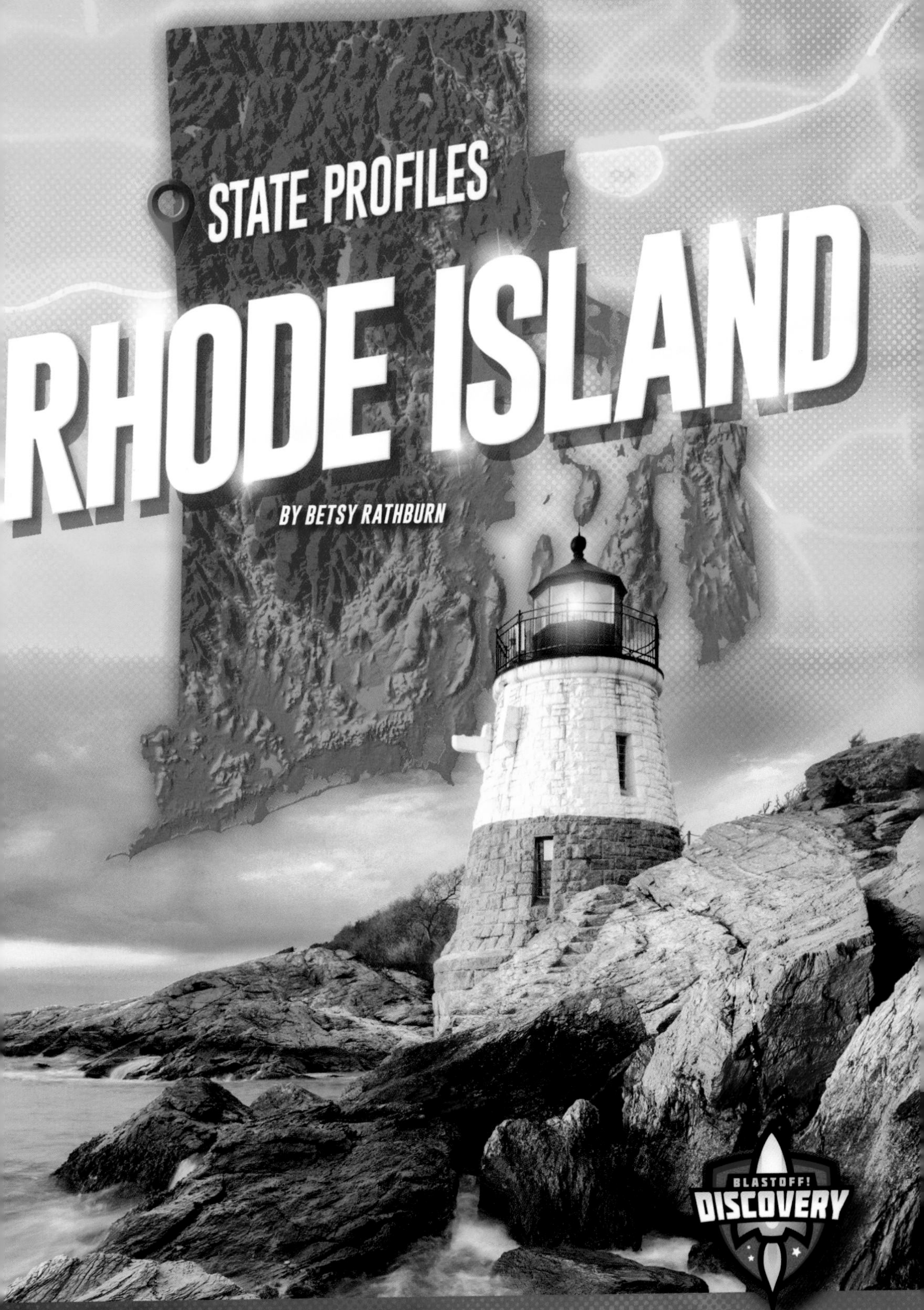

BLASTOFF! DISCOVERY

BELLWETHER MEDIA • MINNEAPOLIS, MN

Blastoff! Discovery launches a new mission: reading to learn. Filled with facts and features, each book offers you an exciting new world to explore!

BLASTOFF! UNIVERSE

BLASTOFF! Beginners — GRADE K

BLASTOFF! READERS — GRADES 1-3

BLASTOFF! DISCOVERY — GRADE 4

This edition first published in 2022 by Bellwether Media, Inc.

No part of this publication may be reproduced in whole or in part without written permission of the publisher.
For information regarding permission, write to Bellwether Media, Inc., Attention: Permissions Department,
6012 Blue Circle Drive, Minnetonka, MN 55343.

Library of Congress Cataloging-in-Publication Data

Names: Rathburn, Betsy, author.
Title: Rhode Island / by Betsy Rathburn.
Description: Minneapolis, MN : Bellwether Media, Inc., 2022. |
Series: Blastoff! Discovery: State profiles | Includes bibliographical references and index. | Audience: Ages 7-13 | Audience: Grades 4-6 |
Summary: "Engaging images accompany information about Rhode Island. The combination of high-interest subject matter and narrative text is intended for students in grades 3 through 8"– Provided by publisher.
Identifiers: LCCN 2021020852 (print) | LCCN 2021020853 (ebook) | ISBN 9781644873458 (library binding) | ISBN 9781648341885 (ebook)
Subjects: LCSH: Rhode Island–Juvenile literature.
Classification: LCC F79.3 .R37 2022 (print) | LCC F79.3 (ebook) | DDC 974.5–dc23
LC record available at https://lccn.loc.gov/2021020852
LC ebook record available at https://lccn.loc.gov/2021020853

Editor: Colleen Sexton   Designer: Jeffrey Kollock

Printed in the United States of America, North Mankato, MN.

TABLE OF CONTENTS

THE FIRST

To locals, Easton's Beach is known as First Beach. It is the first and largest in a line of public beaches along Newport's eastern shore.

EASTON'S BEACH
NEWPORT

A family spreads towels on the sand under a wide umbrella. Time for a day at the beach! The family is spending a summer day at Easton's Beach in Newport. They build sandcastles, collect shells, and swim in the ocean. In the distance, surfers catch waves, and sailboats glide across the water.

BEAVERTAIL STATE PARK

MARBLE HOUSE

MOHEGAN BLUFFS

ROGER WILLIAMS PARK ZOO

The family stops at the snack bar for a treat and takes a ride on the **carousel**. Then they head to the Cliff Walk for a hike. This 3.5-mile (5.6-kilometer) trail offers amazing ocean views. Welcome to Rhode Island!

Rhode Island is a rectangular state in **New England**. This region lies in the northeastern United States. Rhode Island covers 1,545 square miles (4,001 square kilometers). Known as Little Rhody, it is the country's smallest state!

Rhode Island shares its western border with Connecticut. Massachusetts lies to the north and east. The Atlantic Ocean washes upon Rhode Island's southern coast. Narragansett Bay forms part of this shoreline. The state capital, Providence, lies at the northern tip of the bay. Other major cities include Warwick, Cranston, and Pawtucket.

CONNECTICUT

WOONSOCKET

MASSACHUSETTS

PAWTUCKET

PROVIDENCE

CRANSTON

WARWICK

NARRAGANSETT
BAY

RHODE
ISLAND

AQUIDNECK
ISLAND

ATLANTIC OCEAN

N
W + E
S

NARRAGANSETT BAY

Narragansett Bay splits Rhode Island nearly in two. It reaches 28 miles (45 kilometers) inland. More than 30 islands dot the bay.

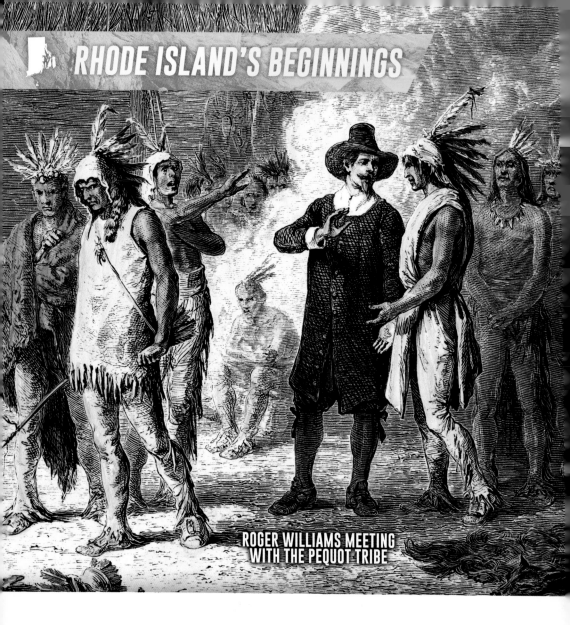

ROGER WILLIAMS MEETING
WITH THE PEQUOT TRIBE

People first arrived in Rhode Island about 10,000 years ago. In time, Native American groups formed. They included the Wampanoag, Narragansett, Nipmuc, Niantic, and Pequot. These peoples lived in **wigwams** and traveled by canoe. They fished, hunted, and grew crops.

Italian explorers reached Narragansett Bay in 1524. In 1636, English **colonist** Roger Williams founded Providence. It drew **settlers** who wanted religious freedom. Rhode Island soon became 1 of 13 English colonies. In 1775, the colonies fought the **Revolutionary War** for their independence. In 1790, Rhode Island became the 13th state to sign the U.S. **Constitution**.

NATIVE PEOPLES OF RHODE ISLAND

NARRAGANSETT INDIAN TRIBE

- Original lands in Rhode Island, Massachusetts, and Connecticut
- About 2,400 in Rhode Island today

POKANOKET TRIBE

- Original lands in Rhode Island and eastern Massachusetts
- More than 200 in Rhode Island today
- Also called Wampanoag

Rhode Island has two main regions. In the west, hills roll across the New England Upland. Forests and lakes cover this area. The state's largest lake is the Scituate **Reservoir**. In the south and east, the land slopes down to the Coastal Lowlands. Much of this region is flat. It features sandy beaches, rocky shorelines, and **lagoons**.

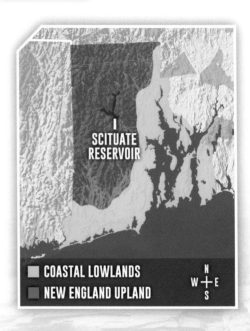

SCITUATE RESERVOIR

COASTAL LOWLANDS
NEW ENGLAND UPLAND

N
W + E
S

TARBOX POND
WEST GREENWICH

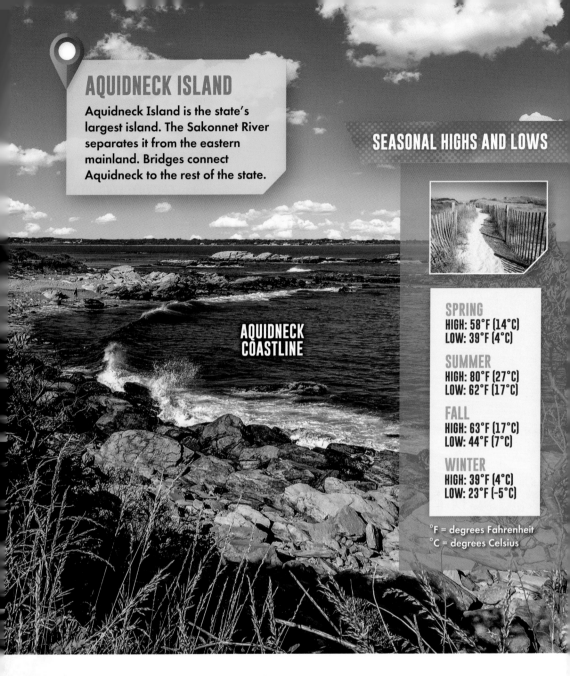

AQUIDNECK ISLAND

Aquidneck Island is the state's largest island. The Sakonnet River separates it from the eastern mainland. Bridges connect Aquidneck to the rest of the state.

SEASONAL HIGHS AND LOWS

AQUIDNECK
COASTLINE

SPRING
HIGH: 58°F (14°C)
LOW: 39°F (4°C)

SUMMER
HIGH: 80°F (27°C)
LOW: 62°F (17°C)

FALL
HIGH: 63°F (17°C)
LOW: 44°F (7°C)

WINTER
HIGH: 39°F (4°C)
LOW: 23°F (-5°C)

°F = degrees Fahrenheit
°C = degrees Celsius

Rhode Island has warm summers and cold, snowy winters. Rain can happen in any season. Sometimes, powerful **hurricanes** bring strong winds and heavy rain.

Rhode Island may be small, but it is home to many different animals! Frogs, turtles, and snakes look for tasty insects around lakes and ponds. Beavers build dams in rivers. White-tailed deer roam forests and fields. Squirrels and chipmunks race through the trees. Blue jays, woodpeckers, and crows perch high on branches.

Seals sun themselves on Rhode Island's coast. Many seabirds live along the coast, too. Gulls and terns pull fish and clams from the salty water. Great white sharks sometimes leap out of the water to catch them! Swordfish, mako sharks, and marlins also swim in Rhode Island's coastal waters.

EASTERN PAINTED TURTLE

EASTERN CHIPMUNK

WHITE-TAILED DEER

MAKO SHARK

LESSER BLACK-BACKED GULL

HARBOR
SEAL

Life Span: up to 30 years
Status: least concern

harbor seal range = ■

LEAST CONCERN	NEAR THREATENED	VULNERABLE	ENDANGERED	CRITICALLY ENDANGERED	EXTINCT IN THE WILD	EXTINCT

▲

More than 1 million people live in Rhode Island. Almost all Rhode Islanders live in cities. It is one of the country's most **urban** states. About four of every five Rhode Islanders have **ancestors** from Europe. Hispanic Americans make up the next-largest group. Asian Americans and Black or African Americans also live in the state. Some Native Americans live in Rhode Island. They include members of the Narragansett and Pokanoket tribes.

CLIFF WALK
NEWPORT

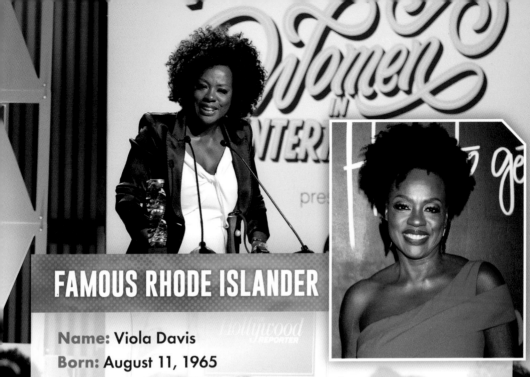

FAMOUS RHODE ISLANDER

Name: Viola Davis

Born: August 11, 1965

Hometown: Central Falls, Rhode Island

Famous For: Award-winning actor, writer, and activist who starred in the movie *The Help*, wrote the children's book *Corduroy Takes a Bow*, and works to stop childhood hunger

Rhode Island has welcomed many **immigrants** in recent years. About one in every eight Rhode Islanders was born outside the United States. Many come from the Dominican Republic, Portugal, and Guatemala.

RHODE ISLAND'S CHALLENGE: A WEALTH GAP

Rhode Island has one of the country's biggest wealth gaps. The state's richest people earn about seven times more money than the state's poorest people. Fixing the gap would help more people lead better lives. It would also help the state's economy.

Rhode Island's capital and largest city is Providence. Founded in 1636, it is one of the oldest cities in the United States! Providence's location on Narragansett Bay helped make it an important seaport. The city also played a large role in the **Atlantic slave trade**.

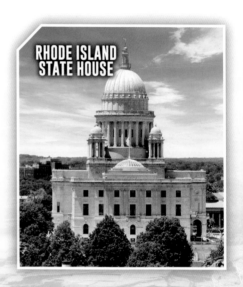

RHODE ISLAND STATE HOUSE

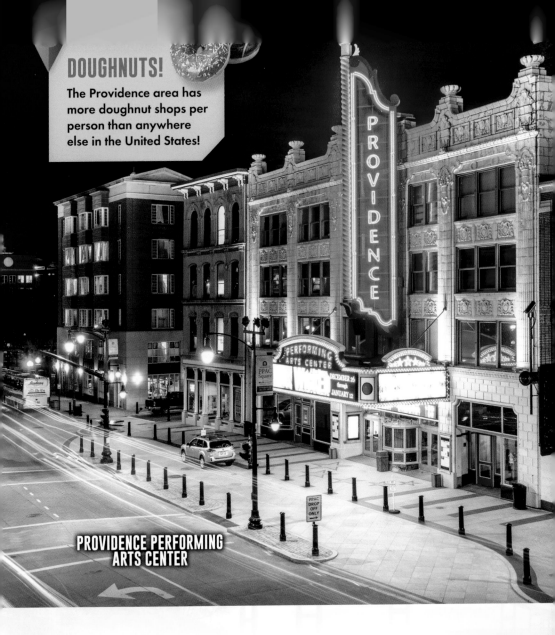

PROVIDENCE PERFORMING ARTS CENTER

Today, Providence is an important **cultural** center. People browse artworks at the Rhode Island School of Design Museum. They see live shows at the Providence Performing Arts Center. Residents head downtown to relax at Waterplace Park. They visit shops and restaurants on the Riverwalk. On WaterFire nights, crowds gather to see the river light up with nearly 100 bonfires!

RHODE ISLAND'S CHALLENGE: UNEMPLOYMENT

Rhode Island has one of the country's highest unemployment rates. A downturn in manufacturing led to many lost jobs. Rhode Island's government must draw new businesses. It can also educate people for new kinds of jobs.

Fishing has long been part of Rhode Island's economy. Today, fishing crews still catch flounder, squids, and scallops in coastal waters. In the early 1800s, Rhode Island became a center for cloth and jewelry **manufacturing**. Today, the state's factories produce medicines, jewelry, and machine parts.

OFFICIAL APPLE

Rhode Island grows a lot of apples! The Rhode Island Greening is the state's official apple. It was first grown in the 1600s.

Most Rhode Islanders have **service jobs**. They work in schools, hospitals, and government offices. Farming is also important. Chicken eggs and dairy products are among the most valuable goods. Rhode Island's soil is poor. Farmers grow most fruits and vegetables in greenhouses.

INVENTED IN RHODE ISLAND

FIRST PRACTICAL AUTOMATIC SPRINKLER SYSTEM

Date Invented: 1881

Inventor: Frederick Grinnell

FIRST TOY COMMERCIAL

Date Invented: 1952

Inventor: Hasbro

MR. POTATO HEAD

Date Invented: 1951

Inventors: George Lerner, Hasbro

DINER

Date Invented: 1872

Inventor: Walter Scott

19

STUFFIES

Many of Rhode Island's famous foods are seafood. Stuffies are a favorite. Chopped clams, bread crumbs, and herbs bake in quahog clamshells. Rhode Island clam chowder features fresh clams in a clear, salty broth. Cooks also serve deep-fried clam cakes with tartar sauce.

A SPECIAL DRINK

Coffee milk is Rhode Island's state drink. It is made by stirring coffee syrup into milk.

Pizza strips are a Rhode Island specialty. Thick pizza dough topped with tomato sauce and cheese is served in big squares. Maple syrup covers fluffy cornmeal pancakes called johnnycakes. Hot wieners are hot dogs with celery salt, mustard, onions, and meat sauce on a steamed bun. For dessert, Rhode Islanders enjoy doughboys. Sugar covers these fried dough pastries.

PIZZA STRIPS

HOT WEINERS

JOHNNYCAKES

12–18 SERVINGS

Have an adult help you make this recipe.

INGREDIENTS

1 cup cornmeal

1 tablespoon sugar

1 teaspoon salt

1 cup boiling water

3 to 4 tablespoons milk

DIRECTIONS

1. Mix the cornmeal, sugar, and salt in a large mixing bowl.

2. Add the boiling water and mix well.

3. Add milk to thin the mixture. It should drop easily from a spoon. Add more milk as needed.

4. Drop the mixture 1 tablespoon at a time onto a hot, greased griddle. Add oil as needed to keep the griddle greased.

5. When one side browns, flip and brown the other side. Serve with maple syrup and butter.

SAILBOAT RACE
NARRAGANSETT BAY

Rhode Islanders make the most of their free time. Crowds fill the stands for Providence Bruins ice hockey games. Sailors race across Narragansett Bay. Rhode Islanders also play soccer and basketball at local parks.

In the summer, Rhode Island's coast is busy with beachgoers. Some try parasailing high above the water! State parks draw campers and hikers. In the winter, some Rhode Islanders enjoy skiing at Yawgoo Valley. Others go ice skating at outdoor rinks. Year-round, residents turn out for museum exhibits, theater performances, and concerts.

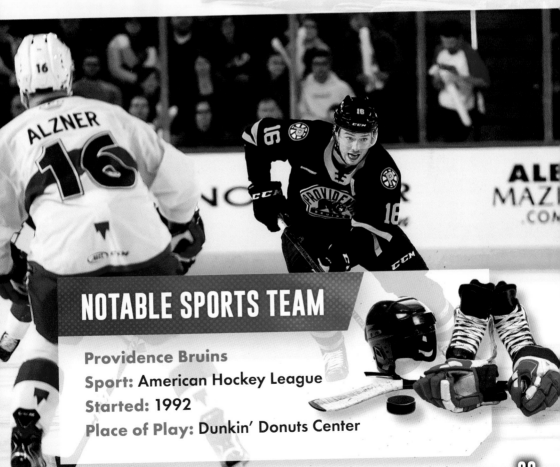

NOTABLE SPORTS TEAM

Providence Bruins
Sport: American Hockey League
Started: 1992
Place of Play: Dunkin' Donuts Center

One of Rhode Island's biggest events is the Newport Folk Festival. Thousands gather to enjoy live music. Bristol hosts the Black Ships Festival each summer. This celebration puts Japanese crafts, martial arts, and foods on display. Puerto Rican Bay Fest in Providence offers food, music, and fun for everyone.

Rhode Islanders also celebrate their favorite foods. Crowds gather at Fort Adams State Park for the Great Chowder Cook-Off. Chefs from around the country offer a taste of their clam chowders. Each August, the Charlestown Seafood Festival serves up freshly caught fish along with music, arts, and crafts. Rhode Islanders have a lot to celebrate!

GREAT CHOWDER COOK-OFF

CLAMBAKES

Every summer, Rhode Islanders throw clambakes. These parties feature a meal of clams, lobsters, potatoes, and corn steamed over layers of seaweed.

NEWPORT FOLK FESTIVAL

1784
Rhode Island begins to ban slavery

1524
Giovanni da Verrazzano explores Narragansett Bay

1696
The Atlantic slave trade begins in Newport

1636
Roger Williams founds Providence

1790
Rhode Island becomes the 13th state

1775–1783
The American colonies fight the Revolutionary War and gain their independence

1794
Rhode Island's jewelry
industry begins

1986
Rhode Island creates
a new constitution

2015
Gina Raimondo
becomes the first
female governor
of Rhode Island

1971
Rhode Island residents
must pay income tax
for the first time

1861–1865
Rhode Islanders fight for the
Union Army in the U.S. Civil War

2012
Superstorm Sandy
hits Rhode Island,
causing millions of
dollars in damage

27

Nicknames: The Ocean State, Little Rhody

Motto: Hope

Date of Statehood: May 29, 1790 (the 13th state)

Capital City: Providence ★

Other Major Cities: Warwick, Cranston, Pawtucket, East Providence, Woonsocket

Area: 1,545 square miles (4,001 square kilometers); Rhode Island is the smallest state.

Population

1,097,379

(2020)

STATE FLAG

Rhode Island's flag was adopted in 1877. It is white with a gold anchor in the center. A blue banner with the state motto "Hope" sits beneath the anchor. Thirteen gold stars surround the anchor and banner. They stand for the 13 original states.

INDUSTRY

Main Exports

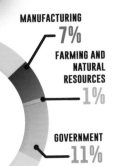

JOBS

- MANUFACTURING **7%**
- FARMING AND NATURAL RESOURCES **1%**
- GOVERNMENT **11%**
- SERVICES **81%**

metal

chemicals

jewelry parts

machine parts

Natural Resources
soil, gravel, granite, limestone

GOVERNMENT

Federal Government

2 REPRESENTATIVES | **2** SENATORS

4 ELECTORAL VOTES

USA

RI

State Government

75 REPRESENTATIVES | **38** SENATORS

STATE SYMBOLS

STATE BIRD
RHODE ISLAND RED

STATE FISH
STRIPED BASS

STATE FLOWER
COMMON BLUE VIOLET

STATE TREE
RED MAPLE

ancestors—relatives who lived long ago

Atlantic slave trade—the transport of enslaved African people to North and South America between the 1600s and 1800s

carousel—a merry-go-round; carousels at amusement parks often feature horses that move up and down.

colonist—someone who is sent by a government to a new region or territory

constitution—the basic principles and laws of a nation

cultural—relating to the beliefs, arts, and ways of life in a place or society

hurricanes—storms formed in the tropics that have violent winds and often have rain and lightning

immigrants—people who move to a new country

lagoons—shallow bodies of water that connect to a larger body of water

manufacturing—a field of work in which people use machines to make products

New England—an area in the northeastern United States that includes Maine, New Hampshire, Vermont, Massachusetts, Rhode Island, and Connecticut

reservoir—a human-made body of water

Revolutionary War—the war from 1775 to 1783 in which the United States fought for independence from Great Britain

service jobs—jobs that perform tasks for people or businesses

settlers—people who move to live in a new, undeveloped region

urban—related to cities and city life

wigwams—dome-shaped homes made with bark or animal skins covering a wooden structure

AT THE LIBRARY

Doak, Robin S. *Exploring the Rhode Island Colony.* North Mankato, Minn.: Capstone Press, 2017.

Heinrichs, Ann. *Rhode Island.* Mankato, Minn.: Child's World, 2017.

Yomtov, Nel. *Rhode Island.* North Mankato, Minn.: Children's Press, 2019.

ON THE WEB

FACTSURFER

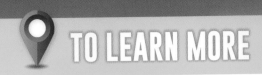

Factsurfer.com gives you a safe, fun way to find more information.

1. Go to www.factsurfer.com.

2. Enter "Rhode Island" into the search box and click 🔍.

3. Select your book cover to see a list of related content.

INDEX

The images in this book are reproduced through the courtesy of: JJM Photography, front cover, p. 9; Ton Bangkeaw, p. 3; KYPhua, pp. 4-5; Wangkun Jia, p. 5 (Beavertail, Marble House); Arena Creative, p. 5 (bluffs); Joe Trentacosti, p. 5 (zoo); North Wind Picture Archives/ Alamy, p. 8; Triana Kidar, p. 10; Karen Lynne, p. 11; Ellen McKnight, p. 11 (inset); E. O., p. 12 (gull); Jay Ondreicka, p. 12 (turtle); Brian Lasenby, p. 12 (chipmunk); Tony Campbell, p. 12 (deer); Xavier Elias Photograp p. 12 (shark); DP Wildlife Vertebrates/ Alamy, p. 13; Thorton Cohen/ Alamy, pp. 14, 24; Stefanie Keenan/ Getty, p. 15; Ga Fullner, p. 15 (inset); M. Unal Ozmen, p. 15 (money); Tupungato, p. 16 (state house); Sean Pavone, p. 16; ESB Professional, p. 17; roundex, p. 17 (fact); Bluegreen Pictures/ Alamy, pp. 18, 22; amomentintime/ Alamy, p. 18 (fact); mipan, p. 19 (sprinkler); jakkapan, p. 19 (commercial); Julie Clopper, p. 19 (Mr. Potato Head); michelabryphoto, p. 19 (fries); Africa Studio, p. 19 (malt); Digihelion, p. 19; Brent Hofacker, pp. 20, 21 (pizza strips, inset, background); gowithsto p. 20 (fact); James Kirkikis, p. 23 (inset); Associated Press/ AP Images, p. 23; Ronnie Chua, p. 23 (gear); Douglas Mason Getty, pp. 24-25; Everett Collection, p. 26 (1636); CPA Media Pte Ltd/ Alamy, p. 26 (1696); Mihai_Andritoiu, pp. 26-32 (background); elen_studio, p. 27 (1794); United States Department of Commerce/ Wikipedia, p. 27 (2015); Wasan Ritthawon, p. 28; Ariene Studio, p. 29 (bird); slowmotiongli, p. 29 (fish); Imladris, p. 29 (flower); Edoardo Palermo, p. 29 (tree); Iakov Filimonov, p. 31.

GEORGIA

BY RACHEL GRACK

BELLWETHER MEDIA • MINNEAPOLIS, MN

Blastoff! Discovery launches a new mission: reading to learn. Filled with facts and features, each book offers you an exciting new world to explore!

BLASTOFF! UNIVERSE

GRADE K

GRADES 1-3

GRADE 4

This edition first published in 2022 by Bellwether Media, Inc.

No part of this publication may be reproduced in whole or in part without written permission of the publisher.
For information regarding permission, write to Bellwether Media, Inc., Attention: Permissions Department,
6012 Blue Circle Drive, Minnetonka, MN 55343.

Library of Congress Cataloging-in-Publication Data

Names: Koestler-Grack, Rachel A., 1973- author.
Title: Georgia / by Rachel Grack.
Description: Minneapolis, MN : Bellwether Media, Inc., 2022. | Series: Blastoff! Discovery: State profiles | Includes bibliographical references and index. | Audience: Ages 7-13 | Audience: Grades 4-6 | Summary: "Engaging images accompany information about Georgia. The combination of high-interest subject matter and narrative text is intended for students in grades 3 through 8"– Provided by publisher.
Identifiers: LCCN 2021019647 (print) | LCCN 2021019648 (ebook)| ISBN 9781644873809 (library binding) | ISBN 9781648341571 (ebook)
Subjects: LCSH: Georgia–Juvenile literature.
Classification: LCC F286.3 .K64 2022 (print) | LCC F286.3 (ebook)| DDC 975.8–dc23
LC record available at https://lccn.loc.gov/2021019647
LC ebook record available at https://lccn.loc.gov/2021019648

Editor: Betsy Rathburn   Designer: Andrea Schneider

Printed in the United States of America, North Mankato, MN.

TABLE OF CONTENTS

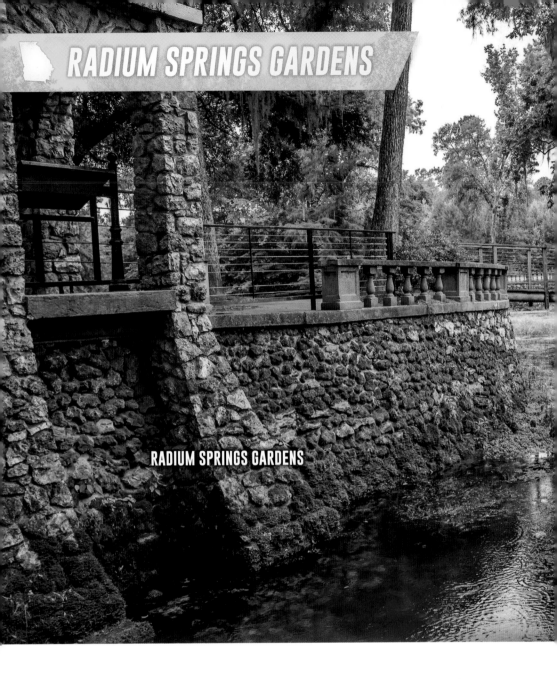

RADIUM SPRINGS GARDENS

A family is spending the day at Radium Springs Gardens. In the courtyard, they stroll beneath broad trees draped with curtains of Spanish moss. Golden sunlight shines through the swaying branches. Along the walkway, butterflies flutter around colorful flowers and budding bushes.

AMICALOLA FALLS

ETOWAH INDIAN MOUNDS STATE HISTORIC SITE

PROVIDENCE CANYON

TALLULAH GORGE

The family stops on a bridge that overlooks Radium Springs. The spring's clear water comes from an underground cave. It is the largest natural spring in the state! In the sunshine, the bright blue-green water appears to glow. Dozens of fish swim through the water. Welcome to Georgia!

TENNESSEE

Georgia is in the southeastern United States. It covers 59,425 square miles (153,910 square kilometers), making it the 24th largest state. Its capital city, Atlanta, sits on the Chattahoochee River in north-central Georgia.

The Chattahoochee River flows west to follow much of Georgia's western border with Alabama. To the north, Georgia shares its border with Tennessee and North Carolina. The Savannah River creates Georgia's border with South Carolina in the northeast. Georgia's southeastern corner touches the Atlantic Ocean. Many islands lie off of the coast. In the south, Georgia shares a border with Florida.

ALABAMA

NORTH
CAROLINA

CHATTAHOOCHEE
RIVER

SAVANNAH
RIVER

SOUTH CAROLINA

N
W E
S

★
ATLANTA

GEORGIA

AUGUSTA

MACON

SAVANNAH

THE GOLDEN ISLES

Four large islands in
southeastern Georgia are
called the Golden Isles of
Georgia. Millions of people
visit their beaches each year!

FLORIDA

REVOLUTIONARY WAR

Native Americans lived in Georgia for thousands of years before Europeans arrived. Around 1540, Spanish explorers traveled through the region. They encountered the Mississippian **culture**. These **native** people were related to the Cherokee and Muskogee, who later lived throughout the state. In the 1830s, most Cherokee people were forced out of Georgia on the **Trail of Tears**.

TRAIL OF TEARS

Georgia was one of the thirteen **colonies** to fight in the **Revolutionary War**. It became the 4th state in 1788. In 1861, Georgia **seceded** from the United States. It fought with the **Confederacy** during the **Civil War**. In 1865, the Confederacy lost the war. Georgia's slaves were freed.

A ROYAL NAME

Georgia was named after King George II of Great Britain.

NATIVE PEOPLES OF GEORGIA

CHEROKEE

- Original lands in Georgia, South Carolina, North Carolina, and Tennessee
- Most relocated in the 1800s
- Around 1,400 members of the Georgia Tribe of Eastern Cherokee today

CREEK

- Original lands in Alabama and Georgia
- Around 2,900 members of the Lower Muskogee Creek Tribe in Georgia today
- Also called Muskogee

The Blue Ridge Mountains cut through northern Georgia. This part of the Appalachian Mountain range is famous for its tree-covered peaks. The Ridge and Valley lies in Georgia's northwest corner. Lines of high ridges rise over long, narrow valleys. The hilly Piedmont region is south of the mountains. It stretches to the coastal **plain**, a region of wetlands that reaches the Atlantic coast.

N
W — E
S

- BLUE RIDGE MOUNTAINS
- PIEDMONT
- RIDGE AND VALLEY
- COASTAL PLAIN

BLUE RIDGE MOUNTAINS
APPALACHIAN MOUNTAIN RANGE

SPRING
HIGH: 75°F (24°C)
LOW: 51°F (11°C)

SUMMER
HIGH: 90°F (32°C)
LOW: 69°F (21°C)

FALL
HIGH: 76°F (24°C)
LOW: 54°F (12°C)

WINTER
HIGH: 58°F (14°C)
LOW: 36°F (2°C)

°F = degrees Fahrenheit
°C = degrees Celsius

GEORGIA'S FUTURE: CLIMATE CHANGE

Climate change affects daily life in Georgia. Flooding causes damage to buildings and roads. Heat waves are dangerous for many people. Over time, this may lead to health problems, unclean water, and poor crops.

Summers in Georgia are hot and **humid**. Thunderstorms and tornadoes often cause heavy damage and flooding. **Hurricanes** sometimes hit the coast in late summer. Winters are short with snowfall mostly in the mountains.

11

Georgia is full of wildlife! Black bears wander through much of the state. Deer graze in grassy fields, while opossums and gray foxes scurry through forests. Owls and hawks perch on high branches. They wait to snatch up chipmunks, squirrels, and gophers. In the wetlands, alligators and water moccasins lie in wait for tasty turtles and birds.

Georgia is home to more than 50 types of salamanders. Pigeon Mountain salamanders scurry through the rocky forests of northwestern Georgia. Georgia blind salamanders hide out in southwestern caves. Southern Georgia's little grass frogs are the tiniest frog in the country. They hop through grassy wetlands in search of insect meals!

GRAY FOX

RED-TAILED HAWK

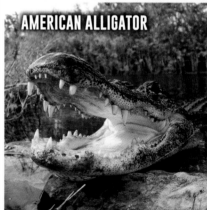

AMERICAN ALLIGATOR

PIGEON MOUNTAIN SALAMANDER

OPOSSUM

WATER
MOCCASIN

Life Span: up to 25 years
Status: least concern

water moccasin range =

LEAST CONCERN	NEAR THREATENED	VULNERABLE	ENDANGERED	CRITICALLY ENDANGERED	EXTINCT IN THE WILD	EXTINCT

Nearly 11 million people live in Georgia. Around three out of four Georgians live in cities. Atlanta is the largest city with over 500,000 residents. Other major cities include Augusta, Columbus, Macon, and Savannah. Georgia is a fast-growing state. Many **immigrants** are moving there. Newcomers arrive from Mexico, India, Jamaica, Korea, and Guatemala.

MACON

A GREAT LEADER

Martin Luther King, Jr. was born in Atlanta, Georgia. His fight for equal rights for Black Americans is famous around the world. He also worked to help poor people and stop wars.

ATLANTA

FAMOUS GEORGIAN

Name: Spike Lee
Born: March 20, 1957
Hometown: Atlanta, Georgia
Famous For: Award-winning filmmaker best known for movies about Black history and culture

More than half of Georgia's population is white. About one out of three Georgians is Black or African American. Smaller numbers of Georgians have Hispanic or Asian backgrounds. There is a small population of Native Americans as well.

GEORGIA'S FUTURE: WEALTH GAP

White families in Atlanta make almost three times more money than Black families each year. Most of the highest-paying jobs are held by white workers. With equal pay, the city's economy would grow.

FORSYTH PARK

Savannah was founded in 1733 by Englishman James Edward Oglethorpe. It was the first city of the Georgia colony. Savannah was a key port for **plantation** products such as cotton and tobacco.

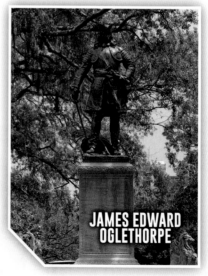

JAMES EDWARD OGLETHORPE

16

Savannah is still a leading Atlantic seaport. It is also a center of culture. Sunbathers stretch out along the beaches of nearby Tybee Island. Families stroll the shady walkways and wide, green lawns of Forsyth Park. The Savannah Historic District is lined with cobblestone streets. People visit to browse shops and eat at the many restaurants. The city is also home to many museums and historic sites.

CITY MARKET
SAVANNAH HISTORIC DISTRICT

PEANUT FARM
DOERUN

Farming has long been important to Georgia's economy. Early plantations grew rice, cotton, peanuts, and tobacco. They relied on slave labor to harvest crops. Later, **manufacturing** became more important. Georgia's cotton production made **textile** manufacturing a major industry.

THE PEACH STATE

Georgia is famous for its peaches. That is why it is called the Peach State!

Today, farming is still important. Georgia is a top producer of peaches, pecans, and peanuts. Factories still make textiles. Paper and processed foods are also important. Georgia's **natural resources** include lumber, marble, stone, sand, and gravel. Almost 8 out of 10 Georgians hold **service jobs**. Many people work in schools, hospitals, or stores.

INVENTED IN GEORGIA

COTTON GIN
Date Invented: 1793
Inventor: Eli Whitney

COCA-COLA
Date Invented: 1886
Inventor: John Pemberton

GIRL SCOUTS
Date Invented: 1912
Inventor: Juliette Gordon Low

ANESTHESIA
Date Invented: 1842
Inventor: Crawford Long

FRIED GREEN TOMATOES

Many of Georgia's favorite foods are grown in the state! Boiled peanuts are often sold at roadside stands. The peanuts are boiled in seasoned water and served warm in their shells. Pecans are made into sweet **pralines**. Georgia peaches may be eaten on their own or baked into peach cobbler.

Grits are a popular Georgia breakfast. Cornmeal is boiled and topped with cheese or fresh shrimp. Brunswick stew is made with meat, potatoes, beans, corn, and broth. Barbecue is also popular. People smoke or roast meat and serve it with a variety of sides. Fried green tomatoes and okra are favorites!

GRITS

BRUNSWICK STEW

PEACH CRISP

6
SERVINGS

Try serving peach crisp with vanilla ice cream! Have an adult help you make this recipe.

INGREDIENTS

4 cups sliced fresh peaches

1/3 cup white sugar

1 cup rolled oats

1/2 cup packed brown sugar

2 tablespoons melted butter

1/2 teaspoon cinnamon

1 beaten egg

DIRECTIONS

1. Preheat oven to 375 degrees Fahrenheit (191 degrees Celsius).

2. Toss the sliced peaches with the white sugar and place in a 2-quart baking dish.

3. Mix oats, brown sugar, butter, and cinnamon together with a fork. Add the egg and mix until well combined.

4. Crumble mixture in small pieces evenly over the peaches. Bake for 35 minutes or until the top is crisp and browned. Serve warm.

21

ATLANTA
FALCONS

Many Georgians love sports! Football fans cheer for the Atlanta Falcons. The Atlanta Braves baseball team draws crowds to their field at Truist Park. The Atlanta Dream and Atlanta Hawks are popular with basketball fans. Soccer fans cheer for the Atlanta United FC.

SAVANNAH BANANAS

The Savannah Bananas are a popular local baseball team. They sell out almost every game!

Many Georgians enjoy hiking in the state's parks or sunbathing on its beaches. People visit Georgia's cities for concerts and other performances. The Tubman Museum draws visitors interested in African American history, art, and culture. The Georgia Aquarium is one of the largest in the world. It has manta rays, beluga whales, and even massive whale sharks!

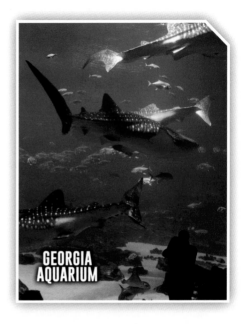

GEORGIA AQUARIUM

NOTABLE SPORTS TEAM

Atlanta Dream
Sport: Women's National Basketball Association
Started: 2007
Place of Play: Gateway Center Arena

Georgia is full of fun events. In March, Macon welcomes spring with the International Cherry Blossom Festival. People gather to celebrate the many pink-petaled cherry trees around the city.

In April, Georgians have a sweet time at the Strawberry Festival in Reynolds. People can try strawberry treats including shortcake, jam, and salsa. The Pan-African Festival is held in Macon every spring. Visitors celebrate the music, food, and art of African and Caribbean cultures. In the fall, the Rockin' Stewbilee is held in Brunswick. The celebration features a stew cook-off and live music. Georgians have plenty to celebrate all year long!

PIG JIG

At the Big Pig Jig in Vienna, Georgia's best cooks compete to roast the juiciest hog!

24

CHERRY BLOSSOMS
MACON

25

1861

Georgia secedes from the United States and joins the Confederacy during the Civil War

1788

Georgia becomes the fourth state

1540

Spanish explorers first travel through Georgia

1733

James Edward Oglethorpe establishes the colony of Georgia with Savannah as the capital

1830s

The U.S. government forces many Cherokee people out of Georgia on the Trail of Tears

1929

Civil rights leader
Martin Luther King, Jr.
is born in Atlanta

1996

Atlanta hosts the
Summer Olympics

1870

Georgia is readmitted
to the United States

2017

Hurricane Irma brings
destruction to Georgia's coast

GEORGIA FACTS

Nickname: The Peach State

Motto: Wisdom, Justice, Moderation

Date of Statehood: January 2, 1788 (the 4th state)

Capital City: Atlanta ★

Other Major Cities: Columbus, Augusta, Macon, Savannah

Area: 59,425 square miles (153,910 square kilometers); Georgia is the 24th largest state.

Population

10,711,908

(2020)

STATE FLAG

Georgia's flag is divided into three stripes. The top and bottom stripes are red, and the middle stripe is white. A blue square in the upper left corner holds the state's coat of arms. Three gold pillars in the coat of arms represent the three parts of government. Banners on the pillars say Georgia's motto. A man with a drawn sword stands between the pillars. Below the pillars is another banner with the United States motto. A ring of 13 white stars surrounds the coat of arms. These represent the thirteen colonies.

INDUSTRY

Main Exports

MANUFACTURING
7%

FARMING AND
NATURAL
RESOURCES
3%

JOBS

GOVERNMENT
13%

SERVICES
77%

frozen poultry

aircraft

wood pulp
and paper

automobiles and
engine parts

Natural Resources
lumber, marble, stone,
sandstone, gravel

GOVERNMENT

Federal Government
14 | 2
REPRESENTATIVES | SENATORS

16
ELECTORAL
VOTES

USA

GA

State Government
180 | 56
REPRESENTATIVES | SENATORS

STATE SYMBOLS

STATE BIRD
BROWN THRASHER

STATE AMPHIBIAN
AMERICAN GREEN
TREE FROG

STATE FLOWER
CHEROKEE ROSE

STATE TREE
SOUTHERN LIVE OAK

GLOSSARY

Civil War—the U.S. war between the Confederacy and the Union that lasted from 1861 to 1865

colonies—distant territories which are under the control of another nation

Confederacy—the group of southern states that formed a new country in the early 1860s; the Confederacy fought against the Northern states during the Civil War.

culture—the beliefs, arts, and ways of life in a place or society

humid—having a lot of moisture in the air

hurricanes—storms formed in the tropics that have violent winds and often have rain and lightning

immigrants—people who move to a new country

manufacturing—a field of work in which people use machines to make products

native—originally from the area or related to a group of people that began in the area

natural resources—materials in the earth that are taken out and used to make products or fuel

plain—a large area of flat land

plantation—a large farm that grows coffee beans, cotton, rubber, or other crops; plantations are mainly found in warm climates.

pralines—candies made from boiled nuts coated in sugar

Revolutionary War—the war from 1775 to 1783 in which the United States fought for independence from Great Britain

seceded—officially withdrew from the United States

service jobs—jobs that perform tasks for people or businesses

textile—woven or knitted cloth

Trail of Tears—the forced relocation of up to 100,000 Native Americans from their homelands to areas farther west in the 1830s; about 15,000 people died on the journey.

AT THE LIBRARY

Hall, Brianna. *Exploring the Georgia Colony*. North Mankato, Minn.: Capstone Press, 2017.

Schwartz, Heather E. *Forced Removal: Causes and Effects of the Trail of Tears*. North Mankato, Minn.: Capstone Press, 2015.

Yomtov, Nelson. *Georgia*. New York, N.Y.: Children's Press, 2018.

ON THE WEB

FACTSURFER

Factsurfer.com gives you a safe, fun way to find more information.

1. Go to www.factsurfer.com.

2. Enter "Georgia" into the search box and click 🔍.

3. Select your book cover to see a list of related content.

INDEX